SHIFTING REGISTERS

Also by Ian Seed

Anonymous Intruder

Shifting Registers

IAN SEED

Shearsman Books

First published in the United Kingdom in 2011 by
Shearsman Books
58 Velwell Road
Exeter EX4 4LD

http://www.shearsman.com/

ISBN 978-1-84861-159-7

Acknowledgements

My thanks to the editors of the following publications where some of
these poems have previously appeared:

*The Argotist Online, Blackbox Manifold, The Café Irreal, Dwang, FIN,
Foam:e, Free Verse, Great Works, Litter, nth position, Pinstripe Fedora,
Poetry Salzburg Review, Poetry Wales, Shearsman, Stride, textVISUAL,
Tears in the Fence,* and *Word for/word.*

Contents

1. Empty either side

2. The only ones awake

3. Each face printed for purchase

'It is much better, I have been advised, just to drift with the stream. The ink washes into a deeper language, and in the end the water runs clear'

—Rosmarie Waldrop

1

Empty either side

Note-taking

Tout cela est matématique
—Flaubert

A bit of heart falls away at the reader's
touch—perhaps a necessary
operating expense after coming so far

through soft rain on a Sunday afternoon
to find the answer is absent in a place
once crowded with strangers. A narrow street

passes endless windows to arrive
at the letterbox whose contours once crossed
the distance between your fingers. A pavement

singer with small hands and a strange
amalgam of narrative postures
fills the puddles with his reflections.

But there's nowhere for them to go, no way
to keep their borders safe when they dissolve,
except on this page, empty and waiting.

Theory

Empty, we can be either side
of the equation when things
go wrong. The perpetual

reverent comes to open
each time in earnest, his face
down to the last card. Light

we pass inside as balloons,
though we must be cautious with
parables and patterns. Best

pierce the order of
symmetry, the sentence truest
when readily lost.

Exterior

Dressed in white fur, almost real
in the distance, her hands repeatedly
enter the river, threadbare yet resistant,
their red mist packed for your disposal.

However lengthily unedited, there's nothing
literal about watching the weightless
train chuff its way through fields of snow,
all the more potent for the shininess

of its invitation to an intimacy
with no future, so that for a moment you think
you have fallen when finally you emerge
from the greasy swathes of steam

to see the island, the real one. But who
is speaking, anyway? My guess is he unbuttons his coat
when you're gone. Better hand back your ticket
and start a new life. I'm right behind you.

This break is the moment

once clear of the town, to measure
a journey between fields, waiting
for us always, each essential
self, as if the act of changing
clothes in the midst of strangers
was a way to say yes. She entered
the tenement building (a central
shaft held all wings and floors), then
she was cleansed. From here the sign
blinked in the distance. There is no
universe like that which bleeds, simply
the structure itself holding
its nose to indicate which
of them doesn't want to die.

One last adventure

Climb the road by the wall
where nobody can hear
how many letters are weighted
above our heads, white
in each binary pair, no one
favoured over another.

By the lake we went,
necessary and tense,
except in darkness your name
lost and multiplied, enough
to drown the story
against its telling

of how I change
on the smoky terrace
and halves melt back together
where your hand touches
or passes into the air
lit up at the edges.

Whatever it is

To enter this foreign city is to re-enter
unending childhood, caught between
fear and expectancy, where the story
still unvoiced but eloquent, is not yet
pegged to the dark tilted foreground
of text on the page.
                    Through the street's
muddy light, giddy as a boy
with brand new pennies in a fairground,
you wander towards the happy end
where *it* will happen, whatever it is
in the emptiness of what was there.

Flipbook

The sequential narrative has started
to disintegrate, setting off
our exploration of glass, mostly
between its pieces. Referring

to the act euphemistically,
how can Miranda do colouring
real and true through the flipbook
of 'alternate realities', or make

'big things' from bright paper
scraps while the boys hide away
in their rooms with a screen
to reshape their faces? But don't

get nervous: here's the canoe
which drifts down the broken river.
We're allowed to admit that we like it
even though it ends in tears.

Resemblances

What kind of face
do I have while leaving
                —Joseph Ceravolo

Even now nothing is certain: my train
is an hour late, and I have to make my way
through faces which multiply and blur
like tears at the end of the platform.

Weightless in front of the toilet mirror,
comb in hand, I try to put myself
back 'in shape', but nothing is solid anymore.
Looking straight into my eyes,

the pupils are too fresh, too fragile
like something which needs to be kept
under glass. And from a distance

here is a man who still hasn't washed
leaning towards me with a blank stare, awaiting
I don't know what deliverance.

Mining the seams

The giant vision that greets us reflects
a tiny figure in shoulderpads. The fusion of the face
with its shadow is total in verisimilitude
beyond the real. It's this story

I always meant to write about one day
in the creamy acreage of buttock and thigh
in a voice that is not quite my own
borne on the winds of the free market,

knowing that whatever I sense in my fingers—
each of which is filled with the same sort of stuff
that connects up to my face—will resist the urge
to touch. Ecce homo: the colour

of his eyes, the shape of his nose
are never the same. For something more lasting,
insert glass eyes into broken skin. What an experience that is,
the mouth filled with a silent cry.

Off-cuts

The door in the corner leads to an empty
stage. They serve up reality in comics
and porn. Our eyes are holes, our noses blotches
which lead to a gaping mouth. Cold thumb-prints
on the skin contain delicate passages and figures
I want to catch. You've got to have a good
frost to make everything die. Sitting up
in bed I can make out the emerging
outlines of foreigners, very thin. Carrying
suitcases has made their hands swell. Soon
they'll be too close not to touch as the whole
city of flesh-coloured work comes into being, evoking
the softness you have entered from. Whose reality
is it anyway? I wish I had a more youthful air
to match the sudden play of light.

Local vicar

Stiff curtains frame children on a country road
who form countless uncertain compounds
and sing of a ladder down into the earth.

I have raised a little animal myself.
But what was the name of the creature—
monkey or dog—with its troubled face

too close to the paper or the window pane?
Though these are insignificant chronicles
they help us understand that death is waiting

while the air of our village blows about.
I can't eat my child, can I? But I can catch hold
of the shadow I have sold. It's a complicated business

knowing when to abandon the excavations for truth
in spite of the clerk's urgent invitation to continue—
an invitation made with a marvellous solitary smile.

Just look what is in it: a daydream of faraway things,
yet real and unquenchable, with something of our childhood
inscribed from the outset, falling finally into place.

Are you receiving?

We're more comfortable paying.
Years ago on an April morning I was once travelling
through and there was only

the borderless green-blue sky, and for moment
ho avuto paura—you can fall
fast and cheap through the unknowns

of algorithms precisely because you don't think
much of maths. What time of day is it?
You lead me to two diagrams

with three overlapping, like ice within.
I'm sitting at the bottom. Do not stain
everywhere you turn from my heart.

You begin to thrive at this trade, a man in dungarees
and a hard hat, your face never
so beautiful. There's nothing wrong

with fixers, but underneath all the whizziness
of the assembly bits there's a child without
a language, fatherless in the suburbs.

We've been too quick, but that Sunday
nobbling the mathematics from behind (the self
divided—again) you wanted it

held. The lightest of winds touched our faces.
Yet when we got home it was all about painting
and perfuming our bodies. *I once lived*

in Milan, you said. *I noticed a lot
of Italian women.* After that opening, we descended
with slippery rhetoric, cashing in where we could.

We thought it was impossible to fall. Too late
I woke to the measureless child. You sported
a tattoo on your cheeks, tackily brilliant.

Opening that self

No crime to tattoo your buttocks. Rather
a way to convert the chronicle of life
into a narrative, or to make a bridge
to the 'not yet', to dismantle the stain
at the centre of your landscape. In the swathes

of its new language, when the rain comes
to wet us, I can call my body mine
with its flesh in the hollow of your heart.
But that doesn't give you carte blanche
to muscle in on what is closed and dark

like the core of some old dream. I can hardly
bear to look at you lying beside me now,
cornily pornographic, or to see the pirate
with his cutlass clear and indelible
digging into your cheek, as if it *were* your cheek.

Quieter than ever

The face disappears with the need to touch
or search for truth, or get lost in the mist
where the chance of being witnessed

is swallowed. Are you there
floating about its edges? While others drift away,
a remembered voice guides our footsteps

though only fleetingly. Through the ambivalence
of architecture in the distance, sky
and sea are bound together. In a cut-out

picture, you blink with surprised
discovery. In the movement down this space
your wave when you turn has no meaning;

yet it is there with the beauty of geometry.
It is you who have changed during
your stroll through the emptiness

between glass buildings where the outlines
of men and women sit unmoving, as if
in a kind of waiting for inner speech.

Not a syllable is heard. We must invent
the hum of wires, the trapped song
of lovers, those faces you will colour later.

Diminishing returns

Light is always seeming to dawn
with its changing shapes in a language
we can never be sure of. The more pages

we turn, the more a different sort of face
emerges with a bright new meaning. The fog's
chalk is rubbed away. Yet still no one can join

the beginning to the end, which is perhaps unknown
even to the narrator, though his professorial voice
ticks on like a clock in an empty lecture hall

in summer—as if it had no means to stop
to drain itself of its own words. His heroine
is endlessly photogenic, yet like a lover's name

traced in steam on a mirror, or a moving figure
in a crowded street, is only visible for a time—
like us, leaving no stain on the air she breathes.

2

The only ones awake

At the border

At the border there is a problem. I am required to show my passport in order to validate the passports of my wife and baby. The officials disappear with it and return only after several minutes, just as our train is about to leave. When I check to see if my passport has been stamped, I find they have exchanged my photo for one of a man on a bar terrace raising a tankard of beer to his lips. It looks like a holiday snapshot, except the photo is faded like that of someone who has recently died. There is no time now to change it back, and I realise I can still use my passport—the face is so unclear that no one will know it isn't me.

In mid-sentence

Sometimes you stop in the middle of a sentence because you have completely forgotten what the beginning of the sentence was and what the end was to have been. Like a man walking in the countryside who shuts his eyes for a moment, then opens them to find himself on a shiny white floor stretching into nothingness. He closes his eyes again but cannot recollect anything of his life. Better perhaps to lie down on the white floor, to curl up and die. Except that here even this possibility does not exist.

Insect

Walking by the council houses in the falling snow, I thought I saw someone waving to me from a downstairs window. Yet when I got close enough to press my face against the frosty glass, I realised I had been mistaken; there was only a family watching television. Looking more closely still however, I saw myself walking on the screen. The youngest daughter was crying because the way I dragged my crushed leg behind me reminded her of an insect.

The only ones awake

We walked up the steep pavement, with each step sinking to our knees in snow. It was past midnight. Holding tight to her hand, I worried that if one of us slipped, then the other would slip too. When we reached the alleyway at the top, I kissed her for the first time. Yet however hard she pressed against me, our thick coats and the silence around us made her seem distant, unreal. The snow started to fall more heavily—huge, curling flakes.

'Don't wake the others!' she whispered. Shivering, naked from the waist down, we lay on our coats on the kitchen floor. I wasn't ready for her, so she pushed me onto my back and sat on me to make it easier. She moved slowly, knowingly. The only part of me that was warm grew inside her.

At the cinema

I sit down in empty darkness. Instead of the film I came for, I see myself on the screen. In silent black-and-white, I am walking along a deserted beach.

Then one by one, they appear, moving without a sound: my mother, much younger, younger than I am, smiling to herself; my sister, her hair in plaits, searching for shells, eleven years old, just as she was when she died; my brother, without his wife and children, puckering his lips in a whistle I cannot hear; my father, the look in his eyes more distant than ever.

One by one, they stop to gaze over the flat, grey sea, seeming not to realise that anybody else is there. I want to shout from my seat, to tell them they are not alone. Yet I'm afraid that if I move or make a sound, the film will disappear.

Ghost story

While he's at his desk, his daughter runs up to him with paper and pencil. She wants him to make a picture for her. He sketches something quickly, without thinking. Since he's awful at drawing, he's surprised at how good the picture is—a big, dark house with all the curtains closed. As he looks more closely, he finds himself inside it. He's standing in the drawing room. A shaft of sunlight pierces the gap between the curtains. For some reason, he thinks of this house as 'my father's house'. But where is his father? Perhaps upstairs asleep or at work in the study. He tries to get his daughter to be quiet. She wants to run around and explore. He wonders why he's never been here before. He didn't know his father lived all alone in such a house.

Through

The surface gleams, but it isn't the colour of the dream. I rise above deep waters, only to find myself cold in the open air. This is what you call entering the world, measured in units of time. Like a child I cannot stop twisting the knobs at the back of the clock. If only I could step into its veins, flow to the tick of its heart. This is the dream unopened. This is what you call fiddling, not coming clean while there's time.

Presences

The wood I have come to is not one I saw on the ordinance survey map. I enter it now in soft grey light.

Sticking through fallen leaves, the broken blade of a plough gleams like something precious.

Where the stream begins, it is iciest, too cold to drink except in drops.

This way please. The man at the fork points me in the right direction. He is utterly certain.

I take the other path, winding and broken.

If it weren't moving, it might be a new tree—that thin figure on the far bank of the river I walk beside.

3

Each face printed for purchase

Still life

Positively there is no chair
down here to offer you
—Joseph Conrad

such slices of the stranger
pushed into a corner
however misty the ending
of climate change
the stack of plastic problems
is part of the fable pattern
for conferring the diagonal
in or out of its shadow
on various rental premises
whose memory is being let
off the lead their forms
planted or returned between the cold
faces across the parapet

it is the same voice in the mouth
just vanished in the curvature
of the red worm then in turn
for symmetry the same breath
a fraction of the expected way
and in those a bridge appears
closer though still unsure
the figures piled everywhere
would find it hard to gather
the elements of the machine
estranged only from its surface
awkward and bluish
floating over real depths

Temps morts

you go into the room to find the old
fashioned summer dress this sense
of bafflement when the stocks tumble

where does the money go dallying
at the edge of a field it remains obdurately
a flower this side of the coin an erotic

escapade everyone a realist the vibration
along the high rises a brightening
search for a meaningful falling

in love work your way up succeeding
dying and so on skyscrapers with tiny
figures on top their jokes in the failed light

we cannot help but feel their dark-blue
coats buttoned with narrative logic
in a bored moment through the filter

of reality we can almost hear the notes
of their old hits shooting up into the sky
they still wear sailor caps don't worry

now it is she who kisses him erode one
get one free in some old field children play
start a fire at the edge of darkness

Risk, and for the present

for Jeremy Over

our olive warning of destruction, moths and flying
                    towards the Italian border
glowed in my hand yet gave off no heat
                    we are safe, but any security
the butcher found pleasant our heads themselves
                    we discover as we go along
the severed insects, the raw meat in our little pocket
                    fearful shapes which
subject to a disease, a night peopled with
                    the pleasure of cutting up
terraces loped all my being, almost everyone
                    between the sky
beautiful as long as it remains untenable
                    scramble to heaven
having loved enough on the light-flooded floor
                    what's it to you
unmade, forced to relocate with the dust of death

Doggedly pretty

the other still exists
                young men meet
poignantly updated
                in geometrical lines
they look skywards
                always at the door
kiss as though no one were looking
                fractures and slants
their apparatus a thin mirror
                turn definite handles
for each to delve into
                and colour distant, odd
erases most of what comes
                turns the same wave
no simple way of knowing
                now disfigured
the face as it enters

Reluctant frames

What do I call the rule by which he proceeds, searching
for missing cows. He is prepared to withdraw and alter them,
at nightfall to find them bombarding one another
for a joke.
        In a part of the country he does not know, he observes
with academic insistence that the path runs in the right direction.
He follows it before he opens his front door. The night's clear
but in the woods it's dark.
                You'll cry with laughter. It's an abyss
more by the sense of touch than sight since you popped your
      eyeballs.
In the direction of your finger, a feeble gleam
swaps parts of his anatomy.
        There is not a single signpost
but this must be the end of the path, where there are chalkmarks
on the ground, though there is no way
to interpret them.
        This window once contained glass
through which you could spot a woman. Her picture,
under-rated, stands roughly here, the fingers push
into the hair
      to help you lose your virginity. A coloured edge
would be more exact. Men break into a dance. Supposing
that we know when no one asks. Perhaps you could stop
for a chat
      in the configuration of the valley, motionless
over the nature of the real sign instead of bellowing
or locking horns. We're unable to repair this torn
skin with our fingers
        even when you unclose your eyes
pointing to home, at the edge of the wood among
the locals, who can say nothing beautiful
of what must lie behind the trees.

Even as we arrive

As yet incomplete, the misery of refurbishment
provides what she wants in the form of a world sheet
whose building blocks grow thickly as in a church.
(She worked first as a model, not a local one.) The point
particles reduce the immense valley to a characterless room
without the protection of extra dimensions. Three
children sick, she wrinkles her nose and orders noodles.

When the calculation is done, the elegance and flexibility
of her approach—the sky low and black over the country—
makes me shoot up taller than the other boys. Throwing
such a ball inside the hose proves testable. The wind
comes in from the sea like a machine gun. Isn't that far away?
An ant crawls inside, very complex, covered in the sweat
of four deserters from a children's ship which is my dream.

Naked, tied to a bed, in another context it might look grubby.
We arrive at the source from different directions as tiny,
vibrating objects. Come here and warm yourself. Early on
when I played the event horizon, I could split and combine
on the street with my companions, well-spoken ladies,
black holes or fuzz balls, emitting and absorbing fifty
voices together and then two or three at a time, enough

to eat in any case. That morning we got up with the rain.
She grabbed my umbrella as I walked along the street.
'The road is not far but where does it end? I'm leaving you
this boat'. There were rules to obey, the ones
we thought had disappeared with the sun.
Lunch was brought in. We thrived on multi-tasking
though we were both afraid of the water, now empty.

Miscast

Into the room by the stair
stinking of blood—a butcher

You stop loving each time
you leave the station with a stranger

We are both in trouble
A disclaimer: these blood vessels

are the deepest
for you have danced so stiffly

in a glade of the little copse
coming in, wet

watching the thin leaves
Twice you've promised to shave

the headless trunk
bored with too much sex

Interrogate the clouds
chop the leaves finely

His own cut has spread
through his massive face

in your lap's softest spot
Do you think it'll rain?

The new song is in the leaves
the young queen on her coin

Bad faith

In this botched sexual encounter
there will be an opening

the otherness of things suffusing the village
with the white of her flickering

thin nostalgia
The same motion bubbles up

as she leaves through the back door
The little strangers, the putative ghosts

with their photo albums
have lost their usefulness

With a baffled and longing face
she has spent her life at home

in familiar rooms with strange colours
where doors are also mirrors

Recent history has slipped away
the ghostwriting is fresh

a body
grim and vinegary

is squashed between surgical axes and wires
She moves quickly to implement blue

she doesn't seem to understand
his sleeves rolled halfway up his forearms

his crisis, the real thing, twice flowering
in the country it depicts

'brainy' things on an iron tray
literally coming through the gates

Feigning interest in sudden savagery
she starts to move away

I've never seen you before, have I
on the road climbing straight into the sky

The real world is there in the silhouettes
of arrivistes in the middle distance

Dante's tree

it flakes off and exposes blood
makes a sea in the ground

trembling in every vein
you open late

from such a small wind you may fall
wash your face

in salt
at high tide

shoulder your pack
the slap of wave up to your knees

you should have known you were in trouble
the deep blue sky, the tinged knife-edge

of sunshine
so simple it has always been like this

but curved outward at the top
farther back many trees

silver-tipped at the window
like some real thing

Tenement ethics

for Ivano Fermini

it's the naked tendons that beget absence
in murky locked territory the years
are entry to the not wanted and ruined
moment then each of the dead doggedly
pretty divides the stream with a nerve
into unexpected meaning a story
of a guest wandering more lips than welcome
with a loss which bodies its curtain
down the shadowy interior rain
unnerves the order of recounted faces
which love logically with their masks
unreliable as the taste of sun the white
self quiets with its editing an abyss
becomes a doorway rubble finds form

Anointing

couldn't find the story   instead came to this
lonely flicker   no one can tell what worth

a hole cut in ice   a mouth of unknown ways
between them   ragged outlines   visible

across the river   rain floating down
in broken design   an entrance

as if this were home   remnant of snow
dull on ledge   might still feel flesh

could melt their mouths   in the same way
to be reborn   between one moment and the next

cover her whole   rain deepening the stone
clean   come to an end   rub your eyes

drop by drop   still dream of falling
never imagine   it will be so kind

Sidestepping grace

1

the documentary skin
spells steep slopes

and other bells
treated as equals

girls
impossible to meet

or kiss in the stairwell
with the notion

of rain hammering the roof
bubbling fat

until midnight
with the light turned off

2

now my estranged
barber

may spot a bald patch soon
blooming in motion

mine is pretty small
in the morning

recentralising
'angels'

no I never saw one
without the inverted commas

which is all she's wearing
her mouth open

3

I creep towards her
ripple

for the rest of the evening
jack it

cradle your jaw
but no less staggering

for its emptiness
delete

in a handkerchief
between the wars

black
with perfect sense

4

a broken wave
no monetary value

thus the rite
whose colour we crave

have you noticed
the smell

behind eyelids
coming down

each face
printed for purchase

numberless
exile

5

as a child I could
with a few sticks

or matches
make part of a face

whatever I wanted
to name without words

nothing resists
on the surface

when I touch
these angels with wings

of paper to cut
or burn

6

images that shrink
or detonate

we are not made in one piece
the machine turns

in emptiness
the way we went down

nor is it important
how we begin to dance

and fragment
in a grainy photo

easy to miss
at first glance

7

dig into sky
to find a heart

people who press
against us with their wings

in a moment
of infinite suggestion

yet I am
of your country

where drops of blood
fall on pavements

indelible
and absolute

Night root

you avoided the moment
with soft thumbs
pressed on nerves underground

a cry then silence
this sudden pulling without now
enter further

a touch unravels the butterfly
bone through skin
their peeled faces

and blurred stars
dream into nails
wake into wings

a child's forgiveness
stains alive
its measure

root over
the smallest
unburnished hand

4

Pressed together through rain

Shifting registers

It's always the same train that can be seen
rushing forward with us inside trying to leave
our selves behind. Their eyes are those
we once shared, and there's something tricklike

about the new, as if nothing had actually changed.
It's we who are the intruders here, shining silvery
like semen on a sheet, spilt onto a geography
of rumples and older stains. Dead tired

we return along the dotted lines, the tunnels which lead
almost to a whole scene, though it takes a while
to recognise each figure and the just visible
colours of hair and eye. And though the whistle

of the train is still relevant, one of us is crying,
looking back through the window, where nothing now
intercepts our view of the distant city, whose perimeters
and dark rooms we once graced as tenants.

Flying colours

At the front door, in startling garb, the chorus
selling gold. But its light is now severely
redimensioned. In any case, you don't need
a ring with me. At the roadside I complete

my notes while the almost-trees go on growing.
The story has changed, our masks no longer etched
into our faces with their lines crossing
and separating like accidental paths.

It may be better to sit this through without hope
of parole. I have prepared myself, knowing
you may not pass this way again. My lips

flicker with absurd precision. It is me who makes
this emptiness, though there is work for you too,
pregnant and empty, always at the beginning.

Le jeu

Is their storytelling ever true?
Or was it always this dirty joke
followed by silence? What

purpose is served by their
account of misfits and fallen
women? Life is trickier

with its vast stock of plots
to steal from. The faithful
light of chronicle only

makes us lonely. Besides
by this time you're already
searching for your keys

in the growing dark, while I
lean into you like the thief
escaped from your favourite tale.

Composition

1

Naked against a background
of darkening blue, the coldness
of their embrace is cinematic:

mimicking multitudes, containing
no one. You can trace the mechanics
with your fingernail

on a window pane—not only
the segments of the act, but the matrix
from which it is removed.

Time now to make your own way
back through the empty gallery. The logic
of the cut is in the space it leaves.

2

Spring may have come already
but your coat feels thin. In the square
they are bent over their stalls.

You move among them, hesitant
like some stray who has wandered
into a picture painted centuries ago.

Your face dissolves when you drop
a coin into the fountain. The scene
may sparkle but you feel

the pull of its undertow. When you settle
at a table, the images swim back
to the surface of a brimming carafe.

3

Bridges criss-cross the city,
trace a picture you cannot
know in its completeness.

Buildings reach down
into the water. So many faces
you will never see again, bodies

pressed together through rain.
Each turning takes you
deeper. Now she asks

if you will turn out the light.
She grows warmer
in your stumbling hands.

4

The streaky reflection seems
more real than the face itself.
In the blue of the eyes

there are questions you would like
to forget, even if this means
wandering without a past.

Yet the picture still exists
when you turn away from it:
a window is lit, a figure leans

at the edge of the darkening
square. Rain makes its own
rhythm on your skin.

Cracks

1

We might have fallen out of the sky. We have only ragged phrases, like children learning to talk.

2

How many streets does it take for a village to become a town? The foreigner will pronounce their names differently, as he walks slowly like a diver at the bottom of water.

3

Children give names to their dolls, whose hearts have beats you no longer hear. They are old from their earliest days— wrinkled, harmless and perfumed.

4

I would like to know where this country begins. I have just left the house.

5

You are mixing paint on an ordinary notepad, a white scar from the woods. It's hard to get the blue out of this sky, isn't it? I'm sorry—is it me or someone else embracing you as you attend to the colour? My hands are full. My fingers are growing.

6

But it isn't *these* things, except for your face. Someone is attending to its shape between two waves. My eye follows the outline of the water, its fingertips.

7

The house is illegible in the rain.

8

So many land down with an exhausted message: he has lost her.

9

Let's dodge this little tree growing out of dust, shall we? Bring me a real flower when I've reached the station, found a place to lie down.

10

In the waiting room, even the smell is familiar, as is the doll abandoned in a corner.

11

All the shadows are alike. He has no idea what it is he turns away from.

12

They hesitate at the edge, wobble before pushing off.

Waking

after Fernando Pessoa

from nowhere
this butterfly
on your sleeping temple

a breeze—the window opens
the faded poster of a princess
flutters on a peeling wall

this breathing
happens
it isn't yours or mine

perhaps in your dream
you face me in the flesh
without a plan to follow

no one will ever join me there
I shan't be able to leave
without crying

you open your eyes
not knowing why
and smile

you've left your dress
outside
in the slow and wavy rain

Erato

for Justyna

Next to me now
in the dark
flesh and skin
skull

and bone
and between
each beat

the silence
of her heart

Picture book
after Wittgenstein

In your book *the world as I found it,* all you've done
is change its shape, as if it were a film
on deep water, or the plan of a town

or a bit of face on canvas. As the landlady says,
it must take care of itself, though she dusts it
weekly and looks at it often.

Suppose I draw a meaningless curve through
this dance of motes in the air and want to report
how I found it. Can a child draw a window

in the *wrong* way? My mistake must be
in waiting for the possibility of truth when
your smile is not quite genuine. I can draw you

a face, but what is it that makes you turn away?
Suppose we were walking by a river? Suppose you pushed me
into its patches of colour? Would you give a reason—

the path you took, a stone, the body of a man,
a bleeding statue as a sign of rain
tomorrow? In the meantime, is the blue

or grey of my eyes to be considered? Will they
be real if I give you the light and shadow
of my body, whose shape you still don't know?

Perturbed conditions

As you see, we repeat the procedure,
isolated and without optical help
or pleasure. We build the fractal air,

see things other eyes don't. The tenets begin
where we describe—humbled
before a form that invades as we enter it,

drawing a blank. Let us take the point
and move unit distance across the *flou*
frank and lively. A gaining

can be made on each hyperplane, the moment
without confines mapped in front of us. Even
by evening, though not exactly in the dark, the shape

shifter leans from the window. Its root
too must be real. One only needs a distraction
strong enough, or perhaps simply something

to laugh about for deviant, formal arrangements
to become shapely in their chains. Fragments of once
coherent bodies may withdraw

now that we have pushed the index open for good. The world
is far away, its shimmering dots of light
fixed in the silence.

Results

Go figure why traffic lights
turn when they do, though
you're probably not thinking
much about maths. Equations

are stacked everywhere
we turn among those
rooting for a breakthrough.
They hope to nobble

the numbers from below. Even
as we grow old, we still
fall back on those who *know*
about maths, with their in-

escapable loaves and fishes.
The weight of their formulas
refuses to drop away
from this odd darkness, where

we have come to hide
and which wishes only
to empty itself of
whatever's been netted.

Fingernails

The lack of them is forgiven.
Unlike spit, they hold
little light. Nothing left

but the dusk. The trouble
begins when the door
of the boarded shop

blows open onto the street
where we used to flaunt
in the sun. Yet however lost

you smile and touch
your scars. There is always
some way to understand:

we can see the fingers
themselves or the shape
of the spaces between them

shift while we wait to be shown
the way, our faces burnt
into the endless wind.

Ghosts

Each room here is a cube
of brightness. Yet the design
comes back quite rimless
and remorselessly monochrome
like someone with all their features
combed back. Flashlights chuckle.
Hey! Your stairs
are dripping. Give me a wave,
make a shape in the window. But this is only
the ocean with its salt returning
under a few painted stars
peeping through clouds, bleaching
our faces white in the darkness
towards the house.

Inference

Here is the illusion of a hill
when you pull the damp sheet
over your shoulder, and say:

bring me a red rose. A rose
is also red in the dark, you say,
and for a moment your cry

—or is it a laugh?—is full
of meaning, like the discovery
of an unused room, or seeing

the word 'true' to be unreal
like a smile on a mask
whose eyes are invisible.

Algebraically

The stranger insists we make this journey,
yet we have much to learn before we can walk
across the room through the glances and gestures

of ghosts who go on reporting their lives
even as I suspend my attempts to capture the flash
of your skirt in narrative. This is too bright, not

a route, you say. Yet it is meshed inside us. I look
at the rose you wear, but am thinking of these colour-
coordinated staff who press behind. This is only

a copy of a journey, you say. We can go no further
without directions of mathematical 'certainty'
where everything fits and can be fanned into life.

Resistance

The crowd moves in the rain with
billiard-ball determinism, until
all its lines are tangled. For a moment

I recognise your face, but I cannot
replicate its look, however hard I try
to paint this picture, in which

glances are exchanged by lovers
while limbs whizz by on the pavement
around them. The hand which paints

becomes a part of the picture,
a story in itself. And here I struggle
at the beginning like a child

who has learnt only one way
of forming letters. For I don't know
what you experience when

I make you stop on the street,
or what you say when you turn
in the rain to speak to me.

Entrance

The stale-sweet smell, warmth
from the back of your neck.
I don't know how to give you

any peace. At the top of the stairs
you take my hand. *I'm not dead—*
I'm here. This is the door

but it isn't open to strangers.
When I look back, it's like peeping
through a keyhole. The shirt

falls away from your
shoulders. You bend over me
until the room disappears.

An interpretation

You've shown me a photo:
a boy with a dirty blazer sits

in the sun. When I say it's you,
you have to think about it first.

Trying to fit your new shape
onto the old one isn't easy.

Is this hand yours? You stare
ahead, as if watching a film

in the dark, where a smile
isn't so noticeable, dreaming

perhaps how all the bits
of a life can be collected

in a single scrapbook. Okay,
come on over and swap.

Lightning Source UK Ltd.
Milton Keynes UK
19 March 2011